DATE DUE

FE 10 '98		
AP 29 '98		
MY 6 '98		
SE 8 '98		
NO 10 '98		
DE 17 '01		
AP 1 '02		
OC 8 '02		
MY 9 '03		
OCT 1 6 2003		
MAR 1 5 2004		
MAR 2 9 2004		
APR 6 2004		
APR 2 2 2005		
MAY 0 1		

DEMCO 38-297

Anoles

by W. P. Mara

CAPSTONE PRESS

MANKATO, MINNESOTA

C A P S T O N E   P R E S S

818 North Willow Street • Mankato, Minnesota 56001

Printed in the United States of America.

Library of Congress Cataloging-in-Publication Data
Mara, W. P.
    Anoles/by William P. Mara
    p. cm.
    Includes bibliographical references and index.
    Summary: Describes the physical characteristics, habitat, and behavior of the anole lizard
        ISBN 1-56065-425-2
        1. Anoles--Juvenile literature. [1. Anoles.] I. Title.
QL666.L25M356 1996
597.95--dc20

                                         96-20748
                                            CIP
                                             AC

Photo credits
R.D. Bartlett, 14-20, 25-28, 34, 43, 47. W.P. Mara, cover, 4, 12, 22, 32, 39, 45. James P. Rowan, 6, 10, 30, 37.

Table of Contents

Words in **boldface** type in the text are defined
in the Glossary in the back of this book.

Fast Facts About Anoles

Scientific Name: Anoles are lizards. They belong to a family called Iguanidae.

Physical Features: Most anoles grow to about eight inches (20 centimeters). They have slender bodies and long tails. They are usually some shade of green or brown. Males have a large colorful throat fan called a dewlap. Females have small dewlaps or none at all. Anoles have toe pads with rows of plates called lamellae. They are covered with microscopic hooks.

Reproduction: Anoles mate at almost any time of the year. Females lay eggs, usually one every few weeks during their breeding season. An anole egg is about the size of a pebble. It will hatch in 60 to 90 days.

Daily Habits: Most anoles are active during the day and sleep at night. They spend most of their time in trees and bushes. The males are territorial.

Range: Anoles live in North America, Central America, South America, and the West Indies.

Habitat: Anoles can be found in a variety of habitats. They are most likely to be found in rain forests.

Life Span: Most anoles live from two to four years.

Food: Anoles are **carnivores**. They eat small insects, including crickets, beetles, and flies.

Chapter 1

American Chameleon

Anoles are often confused with chameleons. The green anole found in the southern United States has been called the American chameleon.

This mistake is easy to understand. Both anoles and chameleons have the amazing ability to change color. But they do not look at all alike. And they belong to completely different groups of lizards.

The word anole comes from the West Indian word anoli (uh-NOH-lee). It means lizard.

The green anole has been called the American chameleon.

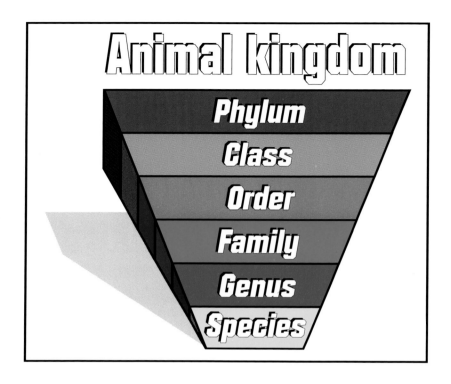

Animal kingdom

Phylum
Class
Order
Family
Genus
Species

Classification System

Anoles are a part of the **scientific classification system**. The system can be thought of as an upside-down pyramid. Animals that are most closely related are at the bottom. The largest animal groups are at the top.

At the very top is a huge group known as a **phylum**. Anoles belong to the Chordata phylum. Just below that is a **class**. Anoles belong to the Reptile class. Then, there is an **order**. Anoles belong to an order with snakes and other lizards. The name of the order is Squamata (skwa-MAH-tuh).

After that, there is a **family**. Anoles belong to the Iguanidae (ee-GWAH-nuh-dee) family. There are smaller groups within the family. Each of these is called a **genus**. Most anoles belong to the genus Anolis. Finally, at the very bottom, is a **species**. There are more than 250 species of anoles.

Common Names

Each anole has its own Latin name and English name. The Latin name is known as the scientific name. The English name is usually called the common name.

Sometimes the common name is based on where the lizard lives. Examples are the Cuban anole and the Crooked Island anole.

Other common names are based on what the lizard looks like. Examples are the big-headed anole, the brown anole, and the stripe-footed anole.

Chapter 2
Where Anoles Live

Anoles live in the southern United States, Central America, South America, and the West Indies. This area is called the anole's natural **range**.

A few other anoles live outside the natural range. The Cuban green anole, for example, is found in Hawaii. But it did not originate there. It came from Cuba in the West Indies. Now it is a normal part of Hawaii's wildlife. It is known as an introduced species or **alien species**.

Anoles are **New World** lizards. Think of the earth as being divided in half, from top to

This anole lives in Costa Rica.

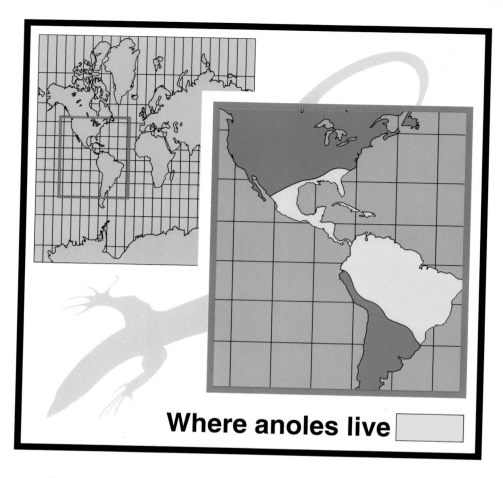

Where anoles live

bottom. The half that contains North America and South America is the New World. The half that contains Europe, Asia, Africa, and Australia is the **Old World**.

Live Near People

Most anoles live in humid places like rain forests. A few anoles live in dry, open forests. Others live around rocks and other shaded, hidden places. Some anoles even live near buildings and roads. There are many anoles living among the residents of Florida.

Scientists believe there is a direct relation between the size of an anole and where it is found within its natural **habitat**. The largest anoles, for example, are usually found near the tops of trees. Those that are slightly smaller are found just below them on the tree trunks or in tall bushes. Finally, the smallest anole species are found close to the ground, at the base of trees or on the branches of low bushes.

Chapter 3

The Anole Body

Anoles range in length from four inches (10 centimeters) to two feet (61 centimeters). Most anoles are about eight inches (20 centimeters) long. Nearly two-thirds of an anole's body length is made up by its tail.

An anole's body is very slender. Such a body is perfect for tree-dwelling. It allows anoles to slip easily between branches and leaves. Also, it is much more difficult for a **predator** to see a thin anole than a fat one.

Most of an anole's length comes from its tail.

Anole Tails

An anole's long tail helps it escape from predators. If a predator grabs the tail, it will break off with little pressure. This is called **autotomy**. The tail bones have cracks in them. The anole uses its muscles to break the bones. The anole runs away and the tail stays behind. The tail continues to thrash for several minutes. While the predator eats the tail, the anole escapes. The anole's tail will slowly grow back. But it will not be as perfect as the original tail.

Most anoles are some shade of green or brown. A few anoles also have shades of orange, yellow, white, black, red, or blue.

The head of most anoles is very thin. Their snouts can be pointed or rounded. Their eyes are small, and they have eyelids. The top of an anole's head can be a different color from the bottom. Anoles have rows of tiny, sharp teeth and strong jaws.

Anole tails grow back if they are broken off.

Colorful Dewlaps

Male anoles have brightly colored throat fans called **dewlaps**. Most of the time the throat fan is folded up under the chin. But the fan comes down when an anole is angry, threatened, or searching for a mate. The unfolded fan is rounded at the bottom, very thin, and usually bright pink. Female anoles have small throat fans. The females of some species do not have them at all.

Like chameleons, anoles can change color. Most can only change between shades of green and brown. A color change indicates a change in an anole's health or mood. Bright colors usually mean the animal is healthy and relaxed. Darker colors indicate the anole feels sick, threatened, or angry.

Some species of anoles need a few moments to make a complete color change. Others can change color almost instantly.

An anole's toes are the key to its ability to hang on to things. On the bottom of each toe are rows of thin plates called **lamellae**. Within

Anole throat fans are called dewlaps.

each of these rows are dozens of tiny hook-shaped cells. The **microscopic** hooks catch in even the slightest irregularities. This allows anoles to crawl on walls, ceilings, and even smooth surfaces like mirrors and window panes. Anoles also have claws that help them climb trees.

Chapter 4
Daily Life

Most anoles sleep during the night and are active during the day. This means they are diurnal. Animals that are active during the night and sleep during the day are nocturnal animals.

Anoles spend most of the time in trees and bushes. This is called an arboreal lifestyle. Other animals are terrestrial. That means they spend most of their time on the ground. Animals that live in the water are called aquatic animals.

Anoles spend most of their time in trees.

Basking in the Sun

Like most reptiles, anoles spend a lot of time **basking** in the sun. They do this because they are **cold-blooded**. They need the sun's heat to survive. Their bodies cannot make their own heat. Instead, they have to get their warmth from the sun.

When they are not basking, anoles are often hunting for food. They chase down their prey and grab it between their jaws. Most anoles are fast. Their prey rarely escapes.

Most anoles like to eat crickets, beetles, spiders, and other insects. Larger anoles also eat mice and small reptiles. Some even eat other anoles. When they are thirsty, anoles lick drops of rain or dew from leaves and branches.

Territorial

Male anoles are territorial. This means they are protective of whatever area they consider to be theirs.

If a male crosses into another male's territory, the occupant anole will bob his head up and down and display his throat fan. If the intruder does not

Most anoles eat insects.

leave after a few moments, the anole will try to chase him away.

When an anole feels danger close by, it may try to change its body color or display its throat fan. It might stand its ground and fight. Or the anole might run away.

The knight anole will become very defensive if it sees a snake or something that resembles a snake, like a garden hose or stick. It will turn sideways, raise its back crest, extend its throat fan, and gape menacingly.

Some anoles will stay close to water so they can swim away when they feel threatened. Often they run so fast that when they hit the water they end up running on top of it for a short time.

Anoles change colors when they sense danger.

Chapter 5

Reproduction

At the start of its breeding season, a male anole will spend most of his time in search of a mate. When he finds one, he will bob his head up and down and extend his throat fan. He does this to impress the female.

If another male comes along and tries to impress the same female, the first male may fight him. If the female tries to run away, he will chase after her. After he catches her, he will climb onto her back and bite her neck. Then mating begins.

Male anoles bob their heads up and down to impress females during mating season.

Eye

Body

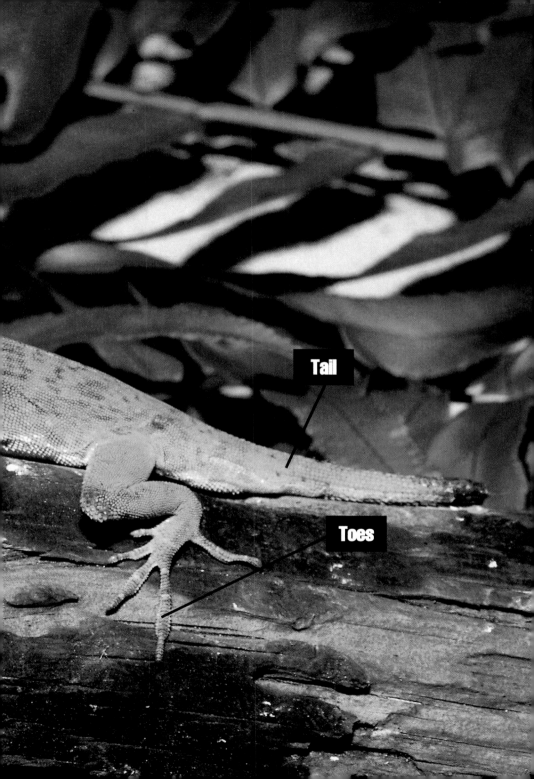

Tail

Toes

Laying Eggs

A few weeks after mating, the female anole will lay an egg. Most anoles lay one egg at a time. They will lay an egg every few weeks during the breeding season. Some other lizards have huge **clutches** of 30 eggs or more.

A mother anole will dig a shallow hole in the ground. She will lay her egg in the hole and then cover it up so it is well hidden. Anoles also lay eggs in leaf litter, rock piles, and moist debris.

Anole eggs are tiny. Most eggs are about the size of a pebble. The eggs will hatch in 60 to 90 days. The baby anoles will be tiny.

After about a year and a half, the babies will be old enough to breed and lay their own eggs. The average lifespan of an anole is two to three years. Some anoles, though, live as long as 16 years.

Female anoles lay their eggs in holes in the ground.

Chapter 6

Conservation

Unlike many animals, anoles are not in any immediate danger of dying out. They are hardy lizards. They have the ability to adapt to changes in their environment.

When a forested area is destroyed to make way for farming or development, the anoles that live there usually will find a way to go on living. It is common to see anoles roaming around places where people live and work.

Groups Help Anoles

Some anole species are rare. Many **conservation** groups try to help anoles and other animals. The animals are protected by

Anoles adapt well to environmental changes.

environmental laws. Rare anoles cannot be taken from the wild and sold as pets. Some zoos keep anoles to breed them and to educate the public about them.

Only a few anole species are sold as pets. Green anoles are popular. People like them because they are easy to keep and fun to watch. They become tame in captivity if they are handled gently. They do best living in large screened cages.

Zoo Trips

If you cannot view anoles in the wild or keep them as pets, visit a zoo. A zoo is a great place to learn about lizards and other animals.

Make the most of your zoo trips. Do not just walk around aimlessly. Leave knowing more than you did before your visit.

Take a notebook with you. When you see a lizard that interests you, stand quietly. Watch the lizard. See what it does. Then write down what you see. You can learn a lot about an animal by doing this.

Side stripes show that this anole is a female.

Ask yourself questions. Is the lizard sleeping during the day? If so, it is probably nocturnal. Is the lizard in a cage by itself? Then it probably is a solitary animal and does not usually live in a group. How big is the lizard? What color is it? How does it act? You will be amazed at how much you can learn by observation.

If you can, bring a camera with you. A zoo is an excellent place to take pictures of animals. Lizards are beautiful animals. If you are a good artist, sketch pictures during your zoo trip. Photos and drawings of lizards give you visual reminders of your trip. You could put the pictures in a scrapbook and use them later for school projects.

Some of the top zoos in which to view lizards are in Houston, Philadelphia, San Diego, and Washington, D.C. In Canada, two of the top zoos are in Calgary and Toronto. But there are many other wonderful zoos, too. Visit a zoo and enjoy yourself. Trips to the zoo are both fun and educational.

Look for the American anole at the zoo.

Some of the top zoos in which to view lizards:

Black Hills Reptile Gardens
South Highway 16
Rapid City, SD 57701

Calgary Zoo
1300 Zoo Road NE
P.O. Box 3036 Station B
Calgary, AB T2M 4R8
Canada

Houston Zoological Gardens
1513 Outer Belt Drive
Houston, TX 77030

Metropolitan Toronto Zoo
361A Old Finch Avenue
Scarborough, ON M1B 5K7
Canada

National Zoological Park
3001 Connecticut Avenue NW
Washington, DC 20008

The Philadelphia Zoological Garden
34th Street and Girard Avenue
Philadelphia, PA 19020

The San Diego Zoo
Park Boulevard and Zoo Avenue
Balboa Park
San Diego, CA 92103

Look for the Jamaican anole at the zoo.

Glossary

alien species—animal or plant that has been brought into an area outside of its natural range and has managed to establish itself there

autotomy—the reflex action by which a lizard's tail is broken off at a special joint

bask—lie or rest and enjoy a pleasant warmth

carnivore—animal that feeds on the flesh of other animals

class—group of animals or plants that have similar characteristics, ranking above an order and below a phylum

clutch—a nest of eggs

cold-blooded—having a body temperature that changes according to the temperature of the surroundings

conservation—the official care, protection, or management of natural resources

dewlap—flap of skin on the throat of some lizards

family—group of related plants or animals, ranking above a genus and below an order

genus—group of closely related plants or animals, usually including several species

habitat—area in which a plant or animal naturally grows or lives

lamellae—thin plates under the toes of some lizards that enable them to hold on to many surfaces

microscopic—too small to be seen by the eye alone but visible through a microscope

New World—the Western Hemisphere

Old World—the Eastern Hemisphere

order—group of plants or animals that are similar in many ways, ranking above a family and below a class

phylum—one of the larger groups into which plants and animals are divided, ranking above a class and below a kingdom

predator—animal that lives by capturing and feeding on other animals

range—geographical area in which a particular animal is found

scientific classification system—the way all living things are listed and categorized

species—group of plants or animals most closely related in the scientific classification system

To Learn More

Barrett, Norman. *Dragons and Lizards*. New York: Franklin Watts, 1991.

Chace, G. Earl. *The World of Lizards*. New York: Dodd, Mead and Co., 1982.

Gravelle, Karen. *Lizards*. New York: Franklin Watts, 1991.

Heselhaus, Ralf and Matthias Schmidt. *Caribbean Anoles*. Neptune, N.J.: TFH Publications, 1995.

Hunziker, Ray. *Green Anoles*. Neptune, N.J.: TFH Publications, 1994.

Ivy, Bill. *Lizards*. Our Wildlife World. Danbury, Conn.: Grolier , 1990.

McCarthy, Colin. *Reptile*. An Eyewitness Book. New York: Alfred A. Knopf, 1991.

Schnieper, Claudia. *Lizards*. Minneapolis: Carolrhoda Books, 1988.

Smith, Trevor. *Amazing Lizards*. New York: Alfred A. Knopf, 1990.

You can read about anoles in *Reptile Hobbyist* and *Reptile and Amphibian* magazines.

This young blue anole lives in Florida.

Useful Addresses

The Long Island Herpetological Society
476 North Ontario Avenue
Lindenhurst, NY 11757

Minnesota Herpetological Society
Bell Museum of Natural History
10 Church Street SE
Minneapolis, MN 55455-0104

The Nature Conservancy
1815 North Lynn Street
Arlington, VA 22209

Ontario Herpetological Society
P.O. Box 244
Port Credit, ON L5G 4L8
Canada

Rainforest Alliance
270 Lafayette Street
Suite 512
New York, NY 10012

Rare Center for Tropical Conservation
1616 Walnut Street
Suite 911
Philadelphia, PA 19103

San Diego Herpetological Society
P.O. Box 4036
San Diego, CA 92164-4036

World Nature Association
P.O. Box 673
Silver Spring, MD 20918

Look for the big-headed anole at the zoo.

Internet Sites

Herp Link
http://home.ptd.net/~herplink/index.html

Green Anole Care in Captivity
http://fovea.retina.net/~gecko/herps/lizards//an oles.html

Green Anole Fact Sheet
http://www.abdn.ac.uk/~psy152/herps/anoles

ZooNet
http://www.mindspring.com/~zoonet

Anole hatchlings are very small.

Index